Amazing Animals

Bugs

Skip Counting

Logan Avery

Ants work.

10

Grasshoppers jump.

30

Flies land.

40

Bees buzz.

50

Moths move.

60

Beetles crawl.

90

Fireflies glow.

100

Problem Solving

Ladybugs are sitting on logs. Count the logs. Then, count the ladybugs by tens. Write numbers to complete the sentences.

1. There are _____ logs.
2. There are _____ ladybugs.

Answer Key

1. 7

2. 70

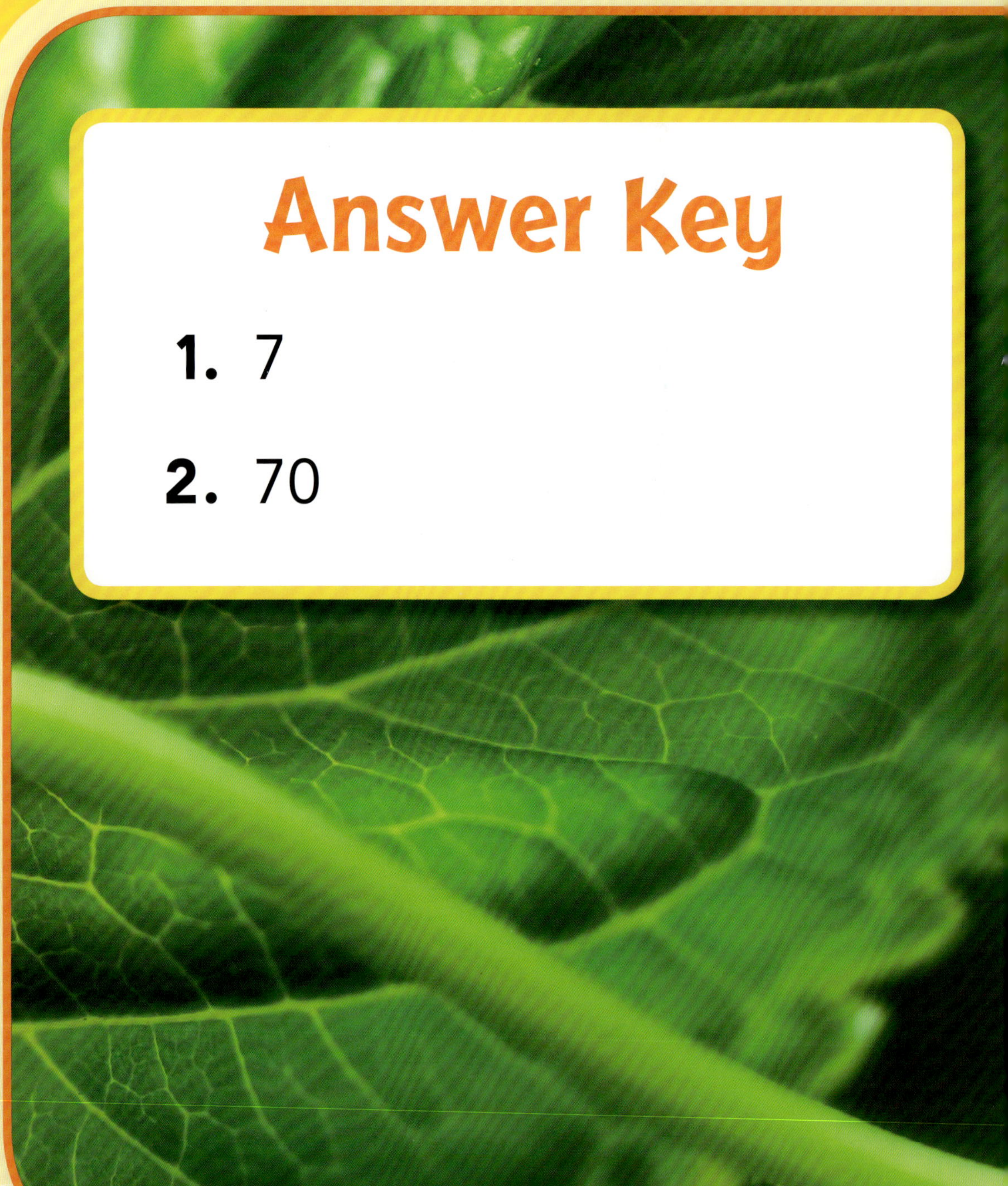

Consultants

Nicole Belasco, M.Ed.
Kindergarten Teacher, Colonial School District

Colleen Pollitt, M.A.Ed.
Math Support Teacher, Howard County Public Schools

Publishing Credits

Rachelle Cracchiolo, M.S.Ed., *Publisher*
Conni Medina, M.A.Ed., *Managing Editor*
Dona Herweck Rice, *Series Developer*
Emily R. Smith, M.A.Ed., *Series Developer*
Diana Kenney, M.A.Ed., NBCT, *Content Director*
June Kikuchi, *Content Director*
Véronique Bos, *Creative Director*
Robin Erickson, *Art Director*
Stacy Monsman, M.A., and Karen Malaska, M.Ed., *Editors*
Michelle Jovin, M.A., *Associate Editor*
Fabiola Sepulveda, *Graphic Designer*

Image Credits: All images from iStock and/or Shutterstock.

Library of Congress Cataloging-in-Publication Data

Names: Avery, Logan, author.
Title: Bugs / Logan Avery.
Description: Huntington Beach, CA : Teacher Created Materials, Inc., [2018] | Series: Amazing animals | Audience: K to grade 3.
Identifiers: LCCN 2017059899 (print) | LCCN 2018008539 (ebook) | ISBN 9781480759510 (e-book) | ISBN 9781425856137 (pbk.)
Subjects: LCSH: Insects--Juvenile literature.
Classification: LCC QL467.2 (ebook) | LCC QL467.2 .A885 2018 (print) | DDC 595.7--dc23
LC record available at https://lccn.loc.gov/2017059899

Teacher Created Materials
5301 Oceanus Drive
Huntington Beach, CA 92649-1030
www.tcmpub.com

ISBN 978-1-4258-5613-7

Printed in China WAI002